mongrel
thumb

CW01082399

Mongrel Thumb presen.

# Eldorado

## by Marius von Mayenburg
### Translated by Maja Zade

Eldorado was first performed in German
at the Schaubühne Berlin in 2004
under the direction of Thomas Ostermeier.

The first performance at the Arcola Theatre Studio 1
on 26 March 2014 is the UK Premiere.

To Caroline and all the Great Clarks
Thank you for your enduring support,
advice, advocacy and encouragement –
they mean a great deal to me. But
above all, thanks for being such
wonderful friends.
With love,
Simon.

arcola
theatre

GOETHE
INSTITUT
Sprache. Kultur. Deutschland.

# Eldorado

by **Marius von Mayenburg**

Translated by **Maja Zade**

CAST

| | |
|---|---|
| Oscar | Nicholas Bishop |
| Anton | Michael Colgan |
| Manuela | Eva Feiler |
| Thekla | Amanda Hale |
| Greta | Sian Thomas |
| Aschenbrenner | Mark Tandy |

PRODUCTION

| | |
|---|---|
| Director | Simon Dormandy |
| Designer | Georgia Lowe |
| Lighting Designer | Matthew Evered |
| Sound Designer | David Gregory |
| Casting Director | Ellie Collyer-Bristow |
| Production Manager | Tamsin Rose |
| Stage Manager | Nicola Buys |
| Assistant Stage Manager | Fern Blevins |
| Set Construction | The Scenery Shop |
| Scenic Painter | Katie Bellman |
| Production Staff | Oliver Welsh |
| | Elliot Carmichael |
| | Elliot Dawes |
| Press Representative | Julia Hallawell |
| Social Media Manager | Jenny Woods |
| Cover Design | Rebecca Pitt – www.rebeccapitt.co.uk |
| Trailer | Dan Pick Video |
| Production Photographer | Zute Lightfoot |
| | |
| Producer | Charles Reston, Gillian Reston and Daniel Brodie for Mongrel Thumb |

We owe the following people and places a great deal of thanks:
Christopher and Sara Reston, Maja Zade, Stage Electrics,
Matthew Evered, Hailz-Emily Osborne and the Farrer Theatre,
Dominic Cooke, Jane Stokes, David Stothard, Andy Fox,
Lee Edwards, Grace Christie at the Duke of York's Theatre,
Damien Hewitt, Becky Wootton, Goethe-Institut London
and all the staff at the Arcola Theatre.

## MARIUS VON MAYENBURG (Writer)

Born in 1972 in Munich, Marius von Mayenburg studied mediaeval literature in Munich and Berlin, and playwriting at the Berlin University of the Arts from 1994 until 1998. In 1998 he began a collaboration with Thomas Ostermeier at the Baracke at Deutsches Theater in Berlin and, from 1999, at Schaubühne am Lehniner Platz, Berlin. He was awarded the Kleist Prize for young dramatists for his first play Fireface (1997) and the Frankfurt Writer's Foundation Prize (1998). Since then, he has written several plays, such as Eldorado, Turista, The Ugly One, The Stone, Perplex and Martyr, amongst others. His plays have been translated into over thirty languages and performed both in Germany and abroad. Since 2009 Marius von Mayenburg has directed several plays at Schaubühne Berlin, e.g. The Pigeons by David Gieselmann, and his own plays Perplex and Martyr as well as the play Call me God, a joint project by the authors Mayenburg, Gian Maria Cervo, Albert Ostermeier and Rafael Spregelburd, at Residenztheater in Munich. Alongside his activities as playwright, dramaturg and director, Mayenburg has translated plays by Sarah Kane, Martin Crimp, Henrik Ibsen and William Shakespeare. Marius von Mayenburg lives in Berlin. In August 2013, he directed his own translation of Shakespeare's Much Ado About Nothing at Schaubühne Berlin and in December 2013, his translation of Oscar Wilde's Bunbury at Residenztheater München.

## SIMON DORMANDY (Director)

As an actor, Simon Dormandy worked with Cheek by Jowl, the RSC, the Donmar Warehouse, and many others. He was Director of Drama and Head of Theatre Studies at Eton College between 1997 and 2012 before turning to directing full-time. He will be directing Waiting for Godot at The Arcola in May and June.

**MONGREL THUMB** (Producer)
Mongrel Thumb, founded by Charles and Gillian Reston, is a brand new London-based theatre company formed out of a love for all things unpredictable, for bringing together seemingly disparate elements to create something challenging, exciting and unique; a one-off. By placing equal importance on emerging artists as on established ones, they aim to mount cutting edge, contemporary productions which will challenge and inspire audiences whilst providing exciting opportunities for the best in up-and-coming talent. Eldorado is their first project.

**MAJA ZADE** (Translator)
Raised in Germany and Sweden, Maja Zade studied at London University, at Queen's University in Canada and at the Royal Academy of Dramatic Art in London. She was Senior Reader at the Royal Court Theatre in London from 1997-99. She is a dramaturg at the Schaubühne Berlin, where she has worked with directors such as Thomas Ostermeier, Katie Mitchell, Volker Lösch, Ivo van Hove, Luk Perceval, Benedict Andrews and Marius von Mayenburg. Her translations into German include works by Lars von Trier, Arnold Wesker and Caryl Churchill, and she has translated works by Marius von Mayenburg, Roland Schimmelpfennig, Lars Norén and Falk Richter into English.

# CAST

**NICHOLAS BISHOP** (Oskar)
THEATRE INCLUDES: A Tale Of Two Cities (King's Head); Moby Dick (Arcola); The Country Wife (Royal Exchange, Manchester); War Horse (West End); The Railway Children (Waterloo Station); Measure for Measure (Theatre Royal, Plymouth); Love's Labour's Lost (Rose, Kingston).
TELEVISION INCLUDES: Doll & Em, Cranford Series II, The Cell II, Banged Up Abroad, Hustle.

**MICHAEL COLGAN** (Anton)
THEATRE INCLUDES: Lulu (Gate/Headlong); Betrayal (Nuffield); King Lear (Everyman, Liverpool/Young Vic/Headlong); Faustus (Headlong/UK Tour); How Much Is Your Iron?, Bedtime Story/The End of the Beginning, This Lime Tree Bower (Young Vic); Blue on Blue (Haymarket, Basingstoke); Hysteria (Northcott, Exeter); Major Barbara, The Playboy of The Western World (Royal Exchange, Manchester); The Cherry Orchard, The Tempest, Amazing Grace (Abbey, Dublin); Ten Rounds (Tricycle); A Midsummer Night's Dream (RSC); Faithful Dealing (Soho); Dolly West's Kitchen (Abbey, Dublin/Old Vic); The Freedom of the City (Abbey, Dublin/New York); Paddy Irishman, Paddy Englishman, and Paddy...? (Birmingham Rep/Tricycle); How I Learned To Drive (Donmar); The Voyage of the Dawn Trader, Animal Farm (Lyric, Belfast); Ripley Bogle (Grace Theatre at the Latchmere).
TELEVISION INCLUDES: Suspects, What Remains, The Thick of It, The Fall, Great Expectations, Midsummer Murders, New Tricks, Doctors, Holby City, Lennon Naked, The Bill, Occupation, Raw, Silent Witness, Soundproof, Animals, Chernobyl, The Year London Blew Up, The Long Firm, Wall Of Silence, Sinners, Sunday, Rebel Heart.
FILM INCLUDES: Heart of Lightness, Good Vibrations, This Is Not a Love Song, The Eliminator.

**EVA FEILER** (Manuela)
THEATRE INCLUDES: The Winter's Tale (Crucible, Sheffield); See What I See (Eyestrings Theatre Company).

**AMANDA HALE** (Thekla)
THEATRE INCLUDES: The Domino Heart (Finborough, Off West End Award Best Actress Nomination); The House Of Bernarda Alba (Almeida); Wastwater, The City (Royal Court); Elektra, After Dido, King Lear (Young Vic); Our Class (National); Pornography (Birmingham Rep/Traverse); The Glass Menagerie (West End, Evening Standard Award Outstanding Newcomer Nomination); Crooked (Bush, Critics Circle Award Most Promising Newcomer Nomination); The Importance Of Being Earnest (Oxford Playhouse).
TELEVISION INCLUDES: Dates, The White Queen, Being Human, Ripper Street, Rev, Crimson Petal And The White, Any Human Heart, Spooks, Murderland, Persuasion, Richard Is My Boyfriend.
FILM INCLUDES: The Invisible Woman, Scrubber, The Look Of Love, Bright Star.

**MARK TANDY** (Aschenbrenner)
THEATRE INCLUDES: Lot and His God (Print Room); Mrs Warren's Profession (West End/Theatre Royal, Bath); Racing Demon (Crucible, Sheffield); The Voysey Inheritance, Luther, The Mountain Giants, Major Barbara (National); Richard II, Beauty and the Beast (Old Vic); Beside Herself, The Lucky Chance (Royal Court); Othello, Merry Wives of Windsor, Julius Caesar, Nicholas Nickleby (RSC); Sweet Panic (Hampstead); Siblings (Lyric, Hammersmith); A Study in Scarlet (Greenwich); The Years Between (Orange Tree Richmond); Reflected Glory (West End).
TELEVISION INCLUDES: Henry IV Parts 1 & 2, Silent

Witness, Silk, Garrow's Law, Minder, Trial and Retribution, New Tricks, The Impressionists, Cherished, Hustle, Space Odyssey: Voyage to the Planets, Alan Clark's Diaries, Shackleton, Darwin, Longitude, The Waiting Time, Arthur, Killer Net, Kiss and Tell, The Buccaneers, A Touch of Frost, Absolutely Fabulous, A Time to Dance, Poirot, Fall from Grace, Portrait of a Marriage, A Vote for Hitler, Inspector Morse, Eye of the Storm, Hedgehog Wedding, The Jewel in the Crown.
FILM INCLUDES: The Deep Blue Sea, Mr Nice, A Cock and Bull Story, Bridget Jones: The Edge of Reason, Claim, The Biographer, The Luzhin Defence, Sophie's World, Mrs Dalloway, Food of Love, Soup, Howard's End, The Railway Station Man, Duel of Hearts, Wings of Fame, Loser Takes All, Maurice, Captive, Defence of the Realm.

**SIAN THOMAS** (Greta)
THEATRE INCLUDES: Passion Play, Up For Grabs (Olivier Award Best Supporting Actress Nomination), Delicate Balance, Kindertransport (West End); Blue Heart Afternoon, The Glass Room (Hampstead); Richard II (Donmar); Brittanicus (Wilton's Music Hall); Who's Afraid Of Virginia Woolf (Northern Stage/Crucible, Sheffield); The Persians (National Theatre of Wales); The Goat (Traverse, Critics Award for Scotland Best Actress Award); Spring Awakening (Lyric, Hammersmith/West End); Small Craft Warnings (Arcola); Fram, House and Garden, Sleep With Me, Richard II, The Way Of The World, Mountain Giants, Square Rounds, The Misanthrope, Countrymania (Olivier Award Best Comedy Performance Nomination), The Wandering Jew (National); Ghosts (Bristol Old Vic); Macbeth, Hamlet, Richard III (RSC/West End); The Price (Tricycle/West End, WhatsOnStage Best Supporting Actress Award); Push Up, Bloody Poetry (Royal Court); Feelgood (Hampstead/West End); King Lear, Happy End, Taming of the Shrew (RSC); The Stronger & The Lover (BAC); Rainsnakes (Young Vic); Private Lives (Royal Exchange, Manchester); Winter Guest (Almeida/West Yorkshire); The Kaisers of Carnuntum Faustina (Arts Carnuntum/Northern Broadsides); The Cutting, China (Bush); Uncle Vanya (UK Tour, TMA Best Actress Award);

The Illusion (Old Vic); Hedda Gabler (Haymarket, Leicester); The Orphan (Greenwich); Pamela (Shared Experience); Othello (Lyric, Hammersmith); Hamlet (Crucible, Sheffield).
TELEVISION INCLUDES: New Tricks, Merlin, The Royal Bodyguard, Syrinx, Thinspiration, Half Broken Things, Lewis, Ruby In The Smoke, Holby City, Vincent, The Last Detective, Midsomer Murders, The Worst Week Of My Life, Crossings, Vanity Fair, Richard II, Blindmen, The Bill, A Mind To Murder, Tears Before Bedtime, Doctor Finlay, Fallen Sons, Wide Eyed & Legless, Taggart, Stanley & The Women, Frankenstein's Baby, After The Party, Victoria Wood Playhouse, Shadow Of The Noose, Inspector Morse, Jury, Maybury, Nancy Astor, Bilylis Blues.
FILM INCLUDES: Harry Potter and the Half Blood Prince, Harry Potter and the Order of the Phoenix, Perfume, Vanity Fair, Rose Red, Erik the Viking, Prick Up Your Ears, Sredni Vashtar.

## CREATIVE TEAM

**GEORGIA LOWE** (Designer)
THEATRE INCLUDES: RSC Trainee Designer (2011-2012), The Linbury Prize for Stage Design (Finalist 2011), The Mystae, Ignorance (Hampstead); Alarms and Excursions (Chipping Norton); Cuckoo (Unicorn); Unscorched, Facts, Fog, Blue Surge, Fanny and Faggot (Finborough); The Ruling Class (English Theatre Frankfurt); Commonwealth (Almeida Festival); Acis And Galatea, Susanna (Iford Arts); Say It With Flowers (Sherman Cymru); LIFT, Shallow Slumber (Soho); The Dark Side of Love (Roundhouse) Pericles, Song of Songs (RSC); Promise (Arts Ed); After The Rainfall (Curious Directive); Yellow (Tête à Tête Opera); Drowning on Dry Land (Jermyn Street); Amphibians (Bridewell).

**MATTHEW EVERED** (Lighting Designer)
THEATRE INCLUDES: La Ronde, The Rivals, Rosmersholm, Julius Caesar, John Bull (Bristol Old Vic); Noises Off, Present Laughter, The Winslow Boy, The Chalk Garden, Spider's Web, The Importance of Being Earnest (Theatre Royal Windsor); King Lear, Joseph K, Three Sisters, The Spanish Tragedy, Henry IV (Farrer); many corporate & commercial events including five Laurence Olivier Awards.

**DAVID GREGORY** (Sound Designer)
THEATRE INCLUDES: Live/Revive/Lament (Aldeburgh Festival); Some Girl I Used to Know (UK Tour); Red Forest (Young Vic/Belarus Free Theatre Company), Our Friend the Enemy (UK Tour & Edinburgh Festival); Midsummer Night's Dream, Comedy of Errors, Pocket Merchant of Venice, The Taming of The Shrew, Twelfth Night, Pocket Henry V, Henry V, Winter's Tale, Comedy of Errors, Richard III (UK, Europe and World Tours/Propeller); eBay Pantomime Cinderella (Charing Cross); Peckham the Soap Opera (Royal Court); Lament (Arcola), Alexandria (Yard); Whisky and Coffee (Oval House); The Physicists (Riverside); Henna Night, Waiting for Romeo (Pleasance); 24 Hour Plays Celebrity Gala, 24 Hour Plays New Voices (Old Vic); The Wages of Thin (Old Red Lion, Off West End Award Sound Designer Of The Year Nomination); Ordinary Lads (ETC); Sudden Loss of Dignity (Bush/Latitude); S-27, The Zoo (Finborough); Strippers And Gentlemen (ICA); An Artist And A Mariner (Minack).

**ELLIE COLLYER-BRISTOW** (Casting Director)
FREELANCE THEATRE INCLUDES: Tape (Trafalgar Studios); Blue Remembered Hills, Playhouse Creatures, Fred's Diner (Chichester); Four Nights In Knaresborough (Southwark Playhouse); Bernarda Alba, Fings Ain't Wot They Used T'Be, Pages (Union); Romeo & Juliet (Chocolate Factory); Bright Lights Big City (Hoxton); Much (Cock Tavern); Naked Boys Singing (Charing Cross); Buddy: The Buddy Holly Story, Buried Child, The Drowsy Chaperone (Upstairs at the Gatehouse); This is How It Goes, A Christmas Carol (King's Head).
THEATRE AS CASTING ASSOCIATE FOR ATG INCLUDES: Dirty Rotten Scoundrels, Macbeth, The Hothouse, The Pride, Passion Play, Spamalot (West End); Blue/Orange, The Rocky Horror Show, Maurice's Jubilee, Tonight's The Night, Annie Get Your Gun (UK Tour).
TELEVISION & FILM AS CASTING ASSISTANT INCLUDES: Come Rain Come Shine, Hattie, Off The Hook, Pimp, Legacy.

Marius von Mayenburg

# ELDORADO

Translated by Maja Zade

OBERON BOOKS
LONDON

WWW.OBERONBOOKS.COM

First published in 2014 by Oberon Books Ltd
521 Caledonian Road, London N7 9RH
Tel: +44 (0) 20 7607 3637 / Fax: +44 (0) 20 7607 3629
e-mail: info@oberonbooks.com
www.oberonbooks.com

*Eldorado* by Marius von Mayenburg © henschel SCHAUSPIEL,
Berlin, 2004, 2014.
*Eldorado* translation by Maja Zade © henschel SCHAUSPIEL
2004, 2014.

Marius von Mayenburg is hereby identified as author of this
play in accordance with section 77 of the Copyright, Designs and
Patents Act 1988. The author has asserted his moral rights.

Maja Zade is hereby identified as translator of this play in
accordance with section 77 of the Copyright, Designs and Patents
Act 1988. The translator has asserted her moral rights.

A catalogue record for this book is available from the British
Library.

PB ISBN: 978-1-78319-136-9
E ISBN: 978-1-78319-635-7

Cover design by Rebecca Pitt – www.rebeccapitt.co.uk

Printed, bound and converted
by CPI Group (UK) Ltd, Croydon, CR0 4YY.

Visit www.oberonbooks.com to read more about all our books
and to buy them. You will also find features, author interviews and
news of any author events, and you can sign up for e-newsletters
so that you're always first to hear about our new releases.

# Characters

ASCHENBRENNER
Anton's boss

THEKLA
mid-thirties

ANTON
mid-thirties

GRETA
Thekla's mother

OSKAR
mid-thirties

MANUELA
early twenties

ASCHENBRENNER: In the distance, beyond the forest, helicopters have ascended, a dark swarm in an echelon formation, they pull up over the city with a shredding drone, teeter over the gasworks, then tilt towards the train station. Shortly afterwards, when the first shots have smashed through the glass roof and sliced open a train standing on the tracks, a black squadron of tactical aircraft cuts through the red sky. It's the beginning of the first wave of attacks. Three months later, we're faced with an extraordinary challenge. Seen from above, the contours of the area resemble a decapitated head. The northernmost point is the veterans' cemetery, where the toppled gravestones appear white against the wreckage of the surrounding area. The smell of burned tropical woods drifts across from the western border: the botanical gardens have burned down to the edge of the riverbank, the orchid house has burst from the heat, and the animals have followed their instincts and abandoned the adjoining zoo. Now they're roaming through the ruins of the government quarter, drinking from the fountains someone has forgotten about, but that's beside the point. By the southern border lies the sports stadium, which has to be conserved in its present condition. When the wind is right, you can hear the refugees' voices ringing out from the oval concrete. If you continue east past the torched wrecks by the side of the motorway, you get to the cadet schools and refineries that were the outermost targets. In the autumn, a murder of crows circles here. Over a total area spanning more than eighty square kilometres, our company is today able to offer you an investment opportunity with unique historic prospects. Here history has entrusted the investor with a piece of the world. A piece of the world that looks almost virginal in the glow of the morning sun.

2.

THEKLA: I just need the garden and a room for the piano.

ANTON: The stairs are for the nursery.

THEKLA: That's news to me.

ANTON: If the tree bothers you we'll get rid of it.

THEKLA: We'll put the barbecue on the lawn and burn sausages, and when it gets loud on the other side of the fence we'll throw water bombs. We need a pergola as well.

ANTON: *(Friendly.)* Yes.

THEKLA: No reason to get into a bad mood.

ANTON: I'm not. Pergola.

THEKLA: Wild wine. And a pond with fish in it. We'll make love on a swinging bench. A birch tree.

ANTON: *(Friendly.)* I don't know when I'll have time.

THEKLA: No need to shout.

ANTON: I'm not shouting, I'm thinking.

THEKLA: We're just getting started. You should be pleased I'm not sitting on the stairs to the nursery, crying.

ANTON: I am. You'll get your birch tree.

THEKLA: It's going to be lovely. A bird just landed in the tree.

3.

ANTON: Please don't destroy me.

ASCHENBRENNER: You've destroyed yourself. You've massacred yourself. Does it bother you when I stare at you like this? You don't have to be polite anymore.

ANTON: If you tell the legal department, you'll blow up my foundations.

ASCHENBRENNER: I don't find this embarrassing. From a professional point of view, you leave me cold. I've sent lots of people to their social deaths without flinching. The only interesting thing about you is my personal failure. That's why I feel sorry for you.

ANTON: I shocked myself.

ASCHENBRENNER: Does the South Pacific mean anything
to you? When I was  there, a lantern-eye fish swam past
my diving mask. His eyes glow when the sea gets dark, so
the small fish, attracted by the iridescence down below,
venture in front of his mouth, and then he closes his teeth
around his prey. You're one of those lantern-eye fish. Your
face is a trap, lethal seriousness shines from your eyes, and
we wander in drunk with naive trust, not noticing your
stupid mouth that shows you're stupid, after all the lantern-
eye fish is related to the slimehead – you've got those
eyes so we don't notice when your stupid mouth snaps
shut. I bet you spend your whole time staring into your
serious eyes in the mirror and hypnotising your brain into
stupidity. Now you're snapping.

ANTON: I have a wife. We're about to buy –

ASCHENBRENNER: Wrong. You're not a cleaning lady. Say
something else.

ANTON: I can't think of anything.

ASCHENBRENNER: Then improvise – isn't that your
specialty? Fake your self.

*(Nothing.)*

Pathetic. I don't mind you underestimating me, your entire
disposition is wrong; your brain is probably a prosthetic.
Here. Sign my name under your dismissal.

ANTON: Where? I don't understand, this is where –

ASCHENBRENNER: I want to see you do it.

ANTON: No no, you're the one who's supposed to –. I see. You
mean, funny, your signature – I'm not that quick, humour-
wise.

ASCHENBRENNER: I don't have a sense of humour. My
signature. So there's a point to you having practised for the
last couple of months. Squeamish? As if it was your first
time.

ANTON: I don't know on what level you want to ruin me now.

ASCHENBRENNER: There aren't many left.

*(ANTON tries to laugh. It's a pathetic attempt.)*

ASCHENBRENNER: *(Shouts at him.)* My signature, slimehead!

*(ANTON signs.)*

ASCHENBRENNER: So you made yourself useful after all. So this is me. You had talent.

## 4.

GRETA: You're beautiful when you've got that stupid look on your face.

OSKAR: I'm looking straight ahead.

ANTON: They tore the palace apart themselves a while ago, they dismantled it from top to bottom, stone by stone, they numbered and filed everything, every column, every statue, all of it.

OSKAR: And then they stored the building in the wine cellar. You're drunk.

ANTON: Not in the cellar. An underground system of bunkers and corridors. Everything was flooded with water, but the basic structure has survived, and they've got the plans, so they can rebuild it just the way it was.

OSKAR: What's this?

ANTON: The ground surrounding the refineries is contaminated, so I'd advise against it. It could take decades.

OSKAR: But it's green.

GRETA: Give me your mouth.

OSKAR: I'm talking.

GRETA: You're chattering. Anton is in politics.

ANTON: I'm in real estate.

GRETA: I want to drink wine and fall into a sexual trance so I can forget this unbearable evening.

OSKAR: I thought it was nice.

GRETA: She's a failure. Where is she, anyway? I hope she's crying.

ANTON: Freshening up.

GRETA: She's taking too much of that stuff, tell her that.

*(To OSKAR.)* And you have no sensuality.

OSKAR: I'm discussing financial prospects. I can't put my tongue in your ear at the same time.

GRETA: I don't mind that you're after my money; I know how to use my assets. My legs are still firm.

OSKAR: And this?

ANTON: That's the street where they hanged people from the lampposts in the transition period. We can't touch the government quarter. I've reserved an appropriate block for you and Oskar.

GRETA: 'You and Oskar.' I just keep him for fun.

OSKAR: That's something.

ANTON: I'm not going to talk you into anything. You're small fry by comparison.

*(We can hear a piano.)*

OSKAR: What's happening?

GRETA: She might as well have put her arse on the keyboard. I feel low.

ANTON: This is what she does when she's messed up a concert. It'll go on all night.

OSKAR: I don't think she messed up. I couldn't do that. All those keys.

GRETA: You're no yardstick. She's hitting the keys, it's like she's playing with hooves, it's an ambush, we're finished.

ANTON: Those are moments of infinite solitude, she's going to punish herself till she gets sore.

GRETA: We're the ones who are being punished, I wonder why, I wore a stole to a community centre and I didn't look at her hands, I've nothing to reproach myself with. Go and put her out of her misery, give her some drops or slam the lid.

ANTON: Sometimes she cries herself to sleep with her face on her fingers.

*(He leaves.)*

GRETA: Tell her to be quiet or I'll come and help her practice.

OSKAR: We shouldn't dilly-dally for too long or we'll lose out on the profit.

GRETA: 'The noble woods are burgeoning with flowers and leaves.'

OSKAR: No.

GRETA: 'Where is the lover I knew?
He has ridden off!
Who will love me?'

OSKAR: Stop it, it's embarrassing.

GRETA: This is an opportunity to show some passion.

OSKAR: I'm supposed to throw you on the cushions now that he's about to walk in with Thekla.

GRETA: I don't like the way you say her name. Get over it. You slid down the stairs on mattresses with her when you were children, but now she's grown up and she wants to play grown-up mattress games. But when she looks at you that doesn't even enter her head. You look like a soft toy.

*(The piano-playing stops.)*

OSKAR: I know where I stand and I'm not going to complain. Stop it.

GRETA: Don't panic, I'm just pulling the stocking over my knee.

OSKAR: I can smell you from here.

GRETA: Then loosen your tie.

OSKAR: What gland is that smell coming from?

GRETA: See if you can find it.

*(OSKAR starts to grope her.)*

OSKAR: You're a gorgeous slut.

GRETA: You're not going to score by being vulgar.

*(THEKLA enters with ANTON.)*

THEKLA: Anton says you've missed me. Doesn't look like it, Anton. What are they doing?

GRETA: Oskar is helping me close my *collier*, which is undone.

THEKLA: I thought he was strangling you.

OSKAR: On the contrary.

THEKLA: Is there a contrary? I know I've got an obscene mother, but when you stroke her she's really sweet.

GRETA: How many did you take?

THEKLA: There's some ice left in the freezer if you want to cool your synapses.

GRETA: Anton, you need to lock that stuff up, look at her.

THEKLA: If you want I can act like a madwoman and throw cactuses around.

GRETA: Maybe if you took the pills before the concert you'd be a bit more gentle with the instrument. Your left hand is a disaster, and I mean well.

*(THEKLA leaves.)*

Your husband says we're small fry.

OSKAR: Where is she going?

ANTON: I said by comparison. We're talking billions here. Multiple digits.

OSKAR: The whole complex is too expensive. We'll go for the west wing, and then we've got sixty percent.

*(We hear the piano again.)*

ANTON: I'll have to check. They're trying to keep the complex together.

GRETA: We'll take the whole thing.

OSKAR: Greta, we're being sensible here.

GRETA: So am I. The whole thing.

OSKAR: We haven't got that much.

GRETA: You don't, that's for sure. We'll take the whole complex, thirty living units and five retail. Don't give me that fishy look, it's not your money. I want a memorial, terraced all the way down to the lower floors, a central life cell with a fountain and an artist's mobile with amplitudes that span several metres in a glass-roof atrium. That's the future down there, it's for the people whose heads they shot through, where there were rapes and ugly details and thousands in tents at the airport. We're going in there with our money and we're paving the way for humanity. It's a positive thing.

OSKAR: I seriously think that you should talk to someone before you do something of this magnitude.

GRETA: My husband's dead. I'm talking to Anton, who is an expert and who has seen their distress.

*(There's a thud, and the piano-playing stops.)*

Dreadful, the way she's hitting the keys.

OSKAR: I think you should consult an independent voice.

ANTON: You can ask whoever you want –

GRETA: He's talking about himself. I'm supposed to let him run the company.

OSKAR: Isn't that why you need me?

GRETA: Everyone knows why I need you.

OSKAR: I won't be reduced to that.

GRETA: You've calculated my prospects. I'm the one who has sole signatory power, you'll have to live with that.

OSKAR: You're only doing this because you want to humiliate me.

GRETA: It's not worth the effort.

*(THEKLA returns.)*

THEKLA: Isn't it time you went to bed?

GRETA: I need your husband in private for a moment.

THEKLA: I don't like it when you make unsavoury remarks. Your mouth is dripping.

GRETA: Anton, tell her to go dig in the garden or something, I want to get through this today.

THEKLA: I hereby announce the end of my career as a solo pianist.

GRETA: Nonsense, go to bed. It wasn't much of a career.

THEKLA: I'm not putting my fingers into that mouth with white elephant teeth anymore. After many long, futile years I'm drawing the line. So that's it. Now you can get the contracts ready.

GRETA: No doubt about it: you're having a crisis.

THEKLA: I tried to break my hand with the piano lid, but I haven't got the guts. Just a swelling.

ANTON: Your precious hands.

THEKLA: Don't want them anymore.

GRETA: You mustn't destroy your hands, they're not yours, they belong to the world, and to art.

THEKLA: The music falls apart in my ears. I can't hear the tune anymore. Just noise. I play the typewriter with so and so many hits per minute. I panic and shoot at everything that moves, it's an unprecedented decline.

OSKAR: *(Takes her hand.)* Squashed and bruised. In terms of organs it's not serious.

THEKLA: You don't know anything. The concert halls are full of assassins these days, if you sit in the balcony you can watch dead people falling into the stalls and then someone turns round and says, 'shush'. They used to shoot them from the box, from behind the curtain, but now they're really laid back, they put the machine gun in the dress circle, in full view of everyone, politely let the audience go past and then shoot when the orchestra starts to play, they shoot the ones they don't need in the rows or on stage, and the smoke rises up into the extinguished chandelier. I've lost the music in all this carnage.

GRETA: Highly strung gestures. There are no boxes or chandeliers where you play. Community centres. You were bad, that's all. We'll start early tomorrow.

ANTON: Leave her alone.

*(To THEKLA.)* I'll put you to bed. I'll sing in your ear and hold my hand over your eyes.

THEKLA: Today I thought the hall was sinking. It tipped over sideways and went under, and everyone in the stalls stayed in their seats when the water rose, and in the end there were toupees floating on the waves and in the balconies the audience applauded the sinking ship. And I sat behind my instrument, my tense fingers sending Morse code to deaf ears. Save our souls. I quit.

ANTON: Sleep. Tomorrow you'll see the world with different eyes.

*(He exits with her.)*

GRETA: *(To OSKAR.)* You're really beautiful when you've got that stupid look on your face. So it's a crisis. Picturesque.

5.

MANUELA: Are you listening?

THEKLA: Every note. Keep playing.

MANUELA: You're looking out the window the whole time.

THEKLA: I should cut some of the branches, the cherries will fall through the open window and onto the carpet.

MANUELA: I feel as if I'm bothering you.

THEKLA: Last night you were crying.

MANUELA: I'm sorry. I thought you couldn't see that from the stage.

THEKLA: At least there was one person in that dumb crowd who was touched. You're talented.

MANUELA: Yes.

THEKLA: Why don't you want to enter competitions? At your age I – how old are you?

MANUELA: It damages one's artistic development.

THEKLA: Aha?

MANUELA: It squanders one's talent ahead of time.

THEKLA: Aha.

MANUELA: Music is not a sport.

THEKLA: Cherry branches look nice in a vase as well.

MANUELA: Ten years from now I don't want to be used up with no hinterland.

THEKLA: But he shouldn't put the flowers on the piano. It feels like we're sitting round a decorated coffin.

MANUELA: I've been wanting to tell you. Can you hear me?

THEKLA: Every note.

MANUELA: I need bigger challenges. The pieces you've been giving me – I can tell from every note what I'm meant to learn. But now it has to be about the music.

THEKLA: It always is.

MANUELA: Great music.

THEKLA: I would have waited another six months.

MANUELA: I'm stagnating.

THEKLA: We can do the Schumann concerto. I don't mind artistic impatience. You have to find your own way.

MANUELA: What I'm trying to say is: I'm not going to do it with you.

THEKLA: And who are you going to do it with?

MANUELA: I don't think there's anything left that I can learn from you.

THEKLA: That depends on you.

MANUELA: What I mean is: I don't think there's anything left that you can teach me.

THEKLA: Aha.

MANUELA: It's not personal. I like you, and I like your garden as well.

THEKLA: I played the Schumann concerto at your age, I won the Liszt Prize.

MANUELA: I know.

THEKLA: I know. It's a long time ago.

MANUELA: You were good for me for a long time, but now –

THEKLA: I'm no longer good enough.

MANUELA: I didn't say that.

THEKLA: And who's better?

MANUELA: I wouldn't like to say.

THEKLA: Christian.

MANUELA: I'd rather not say anything.

THEKLA: Christian is going to mess you up, he's got no ear for you.

MANUELA: I have to find my own way. This isn't easy for me either.

THEKLA: I didn't say this was difficult for me, I've got other students, I'm just sorry about your talent.

MANUELA: It would be nice if we could do this without arguing.

THEKLA: All of a sudden you're a stranger. Only yesterday you sat there and cried.

MANUELA: With pity. It was such a pointless struggle in the community centre. I realised the full extent of your tragedy.

THEKLA: Yes. It really is for the best.

MANUELA: I used to admire you a great deal.

THEKLA: As if I was dead already. You'll have to completely change your technique.

MANUELA: Precisely. That's what it's all about. I still owe you money.

THEKLA: You can call me Thekla if you want. I don't need any authority now.

MANUELA: Thanks. I'd rather not.

### 6.

ANTON: I couldn't get an appointment.

ASCHENBRENNER: That was deliberate. I've no idea what you want.

ANTON: I want my job back.

ASCHENBRENNER: It's not your job and you have no rights. I'll have you thrown out the window.

ANTON: This briefcase is going to help me keep my job.

ASCHENBRENNER: You're standing on a trap door. When I push this button it opens and you slide through the scrap chute down into the canteen waste. Was that clear enough?

ANTON: I'll keep working for you even if you throw me into the potato peels. No one can replace me.

ASCHENBRENNER: Cheeky. You haven't been able to cope with all your free time. You've got rings under your eyes. You need airing. Dissolve an aspirin.

ANTON: I've got the finished contract in this briefcase. A whole complex, with signatures and witnessed, the first instalments are already in my account.

ASCHENBRENNER: You're delirious with fever. I'm going to call your wife and then you're going home to bed with a hot water bottle. You're shattered.

ANTON: My wife isn't stable, she'll jump out the window into the garden with worry. It's one of the complexes by the northern exit road, between the market halls and the bus terminus. We're developing a completely new part of the city.

ASCHENBRENNER: What's the world coming to? Let me take your hand. The city down there is crowded with people. Have you thought about where they're going to detonate the first bombs? There are drawers somewhere in this world that hold plans for the attack, they've even calculated the body count. Have you thought about where you want to be on that morning? Do you want to die in the street, in an exploding car, do you want your head to be crushed by debris from a collapsing house, or do you want a clean shot in the body when you step out of the bakery? Someone else is shaping this city, not you. Go and live in the country. Put turnips in the ground and build a chicken coop. I mean well. This is no place for you. You tried it for a while with my name, but I'm not giving you my chair. It's you or me. And of course it's me, not you.

ANTON: You don't know what you're doing, you're an amateur. You'll go to the dogs.

ASCHENBRENNER: Bundle yourself and your briefcase down into the city. You may take the lift.

## 7.

THEKLA: I'm going to dig up the garden and plant forsythias.

GRETA: Aha.

THEKLA: You look as if there's a collision in your brain.

GRETA: You don't want to take on new students?

THEKLA: I want to pull up weeds.

GRETA: Highly strung.

OSKAR: And in the winter?

THEKLA: Don't know. Maybe I'll grow cactuses with UV light or fly to the equator.

GRETA: I think that's completely deranged.

OSKAR: You're being too radical.

GRETA: She's pumped litres of sweat into her existence, and now she's voluntarily diving back into mediocrity.

THEKLA: I never left it.

GRETA: One snotty-nosed pupil has a tantrum and you sink and deliberately become unfit for society.

THEKLA: Anton earns enough money to feed three families.

GRETA: I know how successful Anton is, that's not the point. *(To ANTON.)* I spent years sitting on the stool behind her waiting for her crooked fingers to reach the octaves.

THEKLA: I want to watch plants grow.

GRETA: But the music.

THEKLA: Doesn't need me. I'll lock the room and bury the key under the compost heap.

OSKAR: None of this is my business, but –

GRETA: *(Interrupting OSKAR.)* Exactly.

*(To THEKLA.)* You need therapy.

*(To ANTON.)* She needs therapy, Anton, common sense won't get us anywhere with her.

THEKLA: I feel better than I've done in years.

GRETA: And that's not normal.

OSKAR: What I was trying to say was: what's so bad about her having a break?

THEKLA: I'm not having a break.

GRETA: She's not having a break. Because if she is she can cross me out of her address book, I don't associate with housewives and gardeners, I won't let her ruin her life just because she thinks it'll hurt me. You're hurting yourself, you stupid cow, you can throw away your career when you have one, when it would cause a scandal and a public outcry, but you're just drowning.

OSKAR: If it's a creative –

GRETA: Shut up. Creative.
    *(To THEKLA.)* I'll give you an address. He can fix this.

    *(Storms off.)*

OSKAR: I'm sorry –

ANTON: Sure, no problem.

    *(OSKAR exits.)*

THEKLA: Don't pull that face, Anton. My personality isn't going to change because of this, and if it does it can only get better.

ANTON: I don't mind your personality.

THEKLA: It's nice that you're being supportive.

ANTON: Thekla, there's something I need to bring up. What you said about me having enough money to feed three families –

THEKLA: I know what you're trying to say: we're not a family yet.

ANTON: No, what I'm trying to say is – our life has to change. Everything will have to be different in the future.

THEKLA: Exactly. It's already different.

ANTON: What?

THEKLA: I'm not just doing this because I'm not talented enough. I went to the doctor's and I'm pregnant.

ANTON: Oh.

THEKLA: We're having a baby.

ANTON: All of a sudden.

THEKLA: Yes. For our nursery.

ANTON: I don't know what to say. I'm shocked.

THEKLA: It's natural that you're deeply moved, you've always wanted this. In the summer we'll blow up a paddling pool in the garden and go strawberry picking in the plantations out of town, in the winter we'll have a fir tree with candles and we'll make biscuits and watch our daughter grow. And the bigger she gets the smaller we'll get until we disappear and everything belongs to her. That's what it's all about, that's the whole purpose, and soon we'll be a part of all that.

ANTON: You've no idea what this means to me.

THEKLA: I love you, Anton. Even more now.

ANTON: I love you too.

THEKLA: What was it you were going to say?

ANTON: Nothing, nothing at all. There's no point now.
Nothing.

THEKLA: Right.

## 8.

OSKAR: Are you watching the lobsters behind the glass?

ANTON: I didn't recognise you with the shopping bags.

OSKAR: Didn't you just come out of that hotel?

ANTON: Me? No. Everything all right?

OSKAR: Couple of errands. Originally I wanted them to kill a
pike, but the catfish had such long barbels that he had to
die instead.

ANTON: The catfish.

OSKAR: I can't get over it.

ANTON: It's just a fish, it doesn't even have warm blood.

OSKAR: I mean, I was sure you just came out of that hotel –

ANTON: Must have been someone else. I look like everyone
else.

OSKAR: And you stare into fishmongers' shops in the middle
of the day? You must be waiting for someone.

ANTON: Me? No. For whom?

OSKAR: You're just watching the lobsters?

ANTON: There's no law against that, is there?

OSKAR: No. I thought you'd be at work, I didn't expect to see
you here.

ANTON: Work, yes, what time is it?

OSKAR: Half past twelve.

ANTON: Right, my lunch break. I often take advantage of my
lunch break.

OSKAR: To watch lobsters.

ANTON: Exactly. They've got rubber bands round their claws, they're waiting for someone to pull them out of the cool water and drop them into a pot filled with boiling broth. It makes me philosophical. In my lunch break. It's relaxing.

OSKAR: Aha.

ANTON: Relieves aggression for the day.

OSKAR: Between you and Aschenbrenner?

ANTON: No no. Personal tension, I keep the office clean.

OSKAR: You must all be in a state of emotional emergency with the region still on fire, the insurgencies, you're very much identified with the project.

ANTON: It's all stable.

OSKAR: I can understand that you seek refuge in these slow, elegant animals.

ANTON: The project is secure, those are the final skirmishes, and with something this big it doesn't matter if a rebel from the north blows himself up somewhere.

OSKAR: So it's not private.

ANTON: What?

OSKAR: I mean you're not looking at moss-covered seafood because there's private tension between Thekla and you?

(ANTON laughs.)

ANTON: You see, I didn't even get that. Not at all. And you're all right? What are you up to?

OSKAR: Yes, a couple of errands. The sad catfish. Dry Riesling. Greta is having a dinner party and I'm cooking, you know what it's like.

ANTON: Not really. Well. I should get going.

OSKAR: Don't you work in that tower at the other end of town anymore?

ANTON: The tower. No, not anymore, we've got a branch office now, I'm now running the branch office.

OSKAR: A promotion.

ANTON: Quasi.

OSKAR: That's nice, Thekla must be proud of you.

ANTON: Yes, very. Very proud, Thekla.

OSKAR: And you really didn't come out of that hotel?

ANTON: I think I'd know. I should go, I've got three men
waiting for me.

9.

THEKLA: You look terrible.

ANTON: My head's buzzing. I slept wrong last night.

THEKLA: All discoloured round your eyes.

ANTON: Mislaid my head.

THEKLA: You whistled in bed.

ANTON: Whistled?

THEKLA: Like this.

*(She whistles.)*

You shouldn't whistle where you sleep, it's rude.

ANTON: It was a rough night, I can't remember.

THEKLA: Makes me want to cry when you're like this. Visiting
from the other side.

ANTON: But I'm nice.

THEKLA: You're terrified. Your work has gnawed at your
bones. He's whipping you into self-abandonment.

ANTON: Who's whipping me?

THEKLA: Aschenbrenner. If you keep working this hard
there'll be nothing left of you. You used to take an interest
in fish.

ANTON: I've had lots of time off since the last deal.

THEKLA: How am I supposed to know, you don't tell me
anything. I can go for days without knowing what you're
up to.

ANTON: I often don't know myself.

THEKLA: I read that there are riots in the government quarter.

ANTON: Thekla, I want to make a deal with you.

THEKLA: What? What does that look mean?

ANTON: Once I've stepped through this door I don't want to hear or say anything about my job. A large part of my brain is always at the office anyway. I'm going gaga. I think in terms of grid squares and field sections. I can't even look at a house without thinking about where they're going to attach the charge to blow it up. In our house the load-bearing wall goes through the bedroom. I want this place to be clear of all that. You're here. I want to look at your beautiful face and not see ruins. I want a safe place. Can you understand that?

THEKLA: Yes. You're pushing me out of your life.

ANTON: No, I want you to pull me into your life, I want to stand under the rhododendron with you and not hear Aschenbrenner's bulldozer in my head, I want to stay sane.

THEKLA: Yes.

ANTON: Can you do that for me?

THEKLA: I'll think about it.

ANTON: I've got three men waiting for me, I have to go.

THEKLA: You haven't eaten anything.

ANTON: I'll have the coffee.

THEKLA: Drink slowly, I'll get your coat.

*(She leaves.)*

You were whistling a march as if it was the Last Judgement. It's ruined my day.

ANTON: As far as I'm concerned it might as well be night, I wouldn't mind giving the dance a miss today. Let's go to bed.

*(Nothing.)*

I said I'm fine, we can skip the day, that's fine with me, and go to bed – oh never mind.

*(Nothing.)*

Did the hallway swallow you up?

THEKLA: There's an odd substance stuck to the carpet.

ANTON: What?

THEKLA: There's something smeared across the hallway.

ANTON: I have to go.

THEKLA: I don't know what it is.

*(ANTON goes to THEKLA.)*

ANTON: Dirt. It's dirt.

THEKLA: In the shape of a trail.

ANTON: I shouldn't have stood up so quickly.

THEKLA: Footprints.

ANTON: I'm going to black out.

THEKLA: From a foot. Don't step in it.

ANTON: My head's buzzing, I need to sit down.

THEKLA: From a shoe. From there to there and into our home.

ANTON: Okay. Let's get rid of the dirt.

THEKLA: Is it dirt? Soil.

ANTON: Whatever it is, I don't want it in the hallway.

THEKLA: Dried and stuck to the fibre structure. Who would bring something like that in here? A sole profile.

ANTON: I think we should –

THEKLA: And here.

ANTON: Should just get rid of it.

THEKLA: Little lumps.

ANTON: Someone is going to end up stepping – and bring it into the house. The dirt.

THEKLA: With fir needles in it. Look, two needles.

ANTON: My head's buzzing. My coffee.

THEKLA: Fir needles. Pines.

ANTON: I'll phone them and they can lather the whole carpet while they're at it.

THEKLA: But we don't even know –

ANTON: Someone walked from there to there. And dropped dirt. I can't get my head round it.

THEKLA: But who, we don't know –

ANTON: I'll phone them.

THEKLA: But –

ANTON: You're not normally like this.

THEKLA: I just want to know, these needles –

ANTON: I'll take care of it. My coffee, I have to go. I've got three men waiting for me.

THEKLA: Maybe the person is still in our house.

## 10.

OSKAR: Anton, we're shocked.

ANTON: It's actually good news.

OSKAR: We bought a concept without old rubble. New rubble if you like, but not a collapsed heritage site.

ANTON: The people that lived there two thousand years ago weren't to know that you want to dig an underground car park there. The tomb is a fact.

OSKAR: But we don't want it. Why don't they just blow away the foundations like the rest of the city?

ANTON: There are enamelled bowls in the ground, armed mummies and even a horse skeleton with gold jewellery.

OSKAR: Cadavers. Great.

GRETA: There are plenty of those anyway.

OSKAR: But none that are two thousand years old –

ANTON: That first night people broke in and ransacked the place.

OSKAR: So then everything's gone and the excavators can start.

ANTON: Now there's a massive military presence securing it. The tomb is a cultural sensation.

OSKAR: A pile of shrivelled corpses.

GRETA: When can we start building?

ANTON: We have to wait till they've dug everything up and shipped it. The planning of the building is more complicated now, they want us to integrate the prehistoric traits. Our proposal is to not plaster the brickwork and to put a glass floor over the vault. The property will be an architectural masterpiece of an international standard.

OSKAR: And twice as expensive.

ANTON: According to our calculations, not quite.

OSKAR: *(To GRETA.)* I told you: the city is dead and dead things stink.

*(To ANTON.)* You've sold us a rotten fish and now you say the rot is special and costs extra and try to sell it to us a second time – at an inflated price. I'm not getting personal here, but that's a scam.

*(To GRETA.)* We'll be throwing more and more money into that hole every year, I warned you from the start, and that's why we're going to sell this money pit as quickly as possible.

ANTON: You can do that, of course. The tourist industry pays triple dollar for property on historic ground. A restaurant with a view of the catacombs –

OSKAR: Who wants to look at that when they're eating?

GRETA: *(To OSKAR.)* Stupid man, you're getting worked up.

OSKAR: Isn't it true?

GRETA: *(To ANTON.)* Send me the new calculation. I'll see the boy home.

OSKAR: I'm going to bite the carpet.

GRETA: If possible with a ground plan for the restaurant.

ANTON: Of course.

GRETA: *(To OSKAR.)* You're beautiful when you've got that stupid look on your face.

OSKAR: You're only doing this to humiliate me.

GRETA: I can afford it.

## 11.

*(MANUELA is playing the piano, ANTON is listening. THEKLA comes home and switches on the light.)*

THEKLA: Who's playing?

MANUELA: Sorry.

ANTON: I was worried.

THEKLA: I was at the doctor's. Why are you sitting in the dark?

ANTON: We were waiting for you.

THEKLA: With no light.

MANUELA: My fault. When I got here the sun was still in the room like when I used to have my lesson.

ANTON: I was worried, she played the piano.

THEKLA: I went to see the doctor.

ANTON: Right.

THEKLA: Why did you open the room?

MANUELA: I missed the view of the cherries. I'm not happy, I want to come back.

THEKLA: Because you miss the cherry tree?

MANUELA: I'm losing everything.

THEKLA: That's normal.

*(To ANTON.)* And you just sit there and listen to her hitting the instrument? It's irritating.

ANTON: That was Schumann. You used to play it.

THEKLA: I know who composed it.

ANTON: Of course.

THEKLA: And?

ANTON: And what?

THEKLA: Does she play well?

ANTON: I can't tell.

THEKLA: Of course her playing is divine. Now there are lots of moths.

MANUELA: Because you switched the light on.

THEKLA: What was I supposed to do with you sitting here in the dark? You look pale. Haven't you managed to sell the government quarter yet?

ANTON: Thekla.

THEKLA: Sorry, it's a secret, I forgot. And apart from that? Spent the day getting mouldy at the office? Or isn't that allowed either?

ANTON: No, the whole time behind my desk.

THEKLA: Overtime?

ANTON: What do you mean?

THEKLA: Sympathy. Because you look green against the window.

ANTON: No, no overtime, I left on time.

MANUELA: Excuse me.

THEKLA: You're still here, excuse me, I was talking to my husband, what was I thinking? Would you like to stay and listen or go home and practise?

MANUELA: I cried all night. I've done everything wrong. Nothing's right anymore, it's not just the piano, suddenly everything's wrong. As if I was stuck in someone else's life. I've lost something and I'm scared I won't get it back.

THEKLA: You lose things as you get older. You must try and cope. I'm getting older myself and putting things behind me – you for example.

MANUELA: I just didn't have anything to compare it with. This is where I belong, here in this room with the tree in the window, I need your heavy perfume and sleepwalker's voice. Christian is ruining me.

THEKLA: Now this creature is crying.

MANUELA: You despise me, I can understand that.

THEKLA: Blow your nose, I'll walk you to the door.

*(She takes MANUELA's arm.)*

MANUELA: The last couple of days I've been breathing, he says my breathing's wrong and he makes me sing, I'm supposed to open up when I'm playing, I need to connect with my shadow-self and immerse myself before I start playing, but I always fall asleep, he says that's a good sign, but it's just that I can't sleep at night because all that breathing is giving me asthma attacks, and I spend the whole night sitting in an armchair coughing. I'm miserable.

THEKLA: I don't think there's anything left that you can teach me. Drink hot milk with honey and say hello to Christian from me.

*(MANUELA has left.)*

ANTON: Poor child.

THEKLA: Highly strung.

ANTON: What did the doctor say?

THEKLA: He put cold goo on my belly and I saw her: a little human being in a blizzard-like typhoon.

ANTON: But what did the doctor say?

THEKLA: He asked where you were and why you didn't want to be with me when we look at the child.

ANTON: I'm sorry, I was working.

THEKLA: That's what I told him, but unfortunately it's not true.

ANTON: Why?

THEKLA: I waited so you could come to the doctor's with me, and I sat in the car in front of the main entrance. You said you didn't work late and you left on time.

ANTON: Right.

THEKLA: But I didn't see you. Aschenbrenner limped out the door on time, doubled over, with a yellow face, as if he was having cramps, I got worried and rang the bell and you didn't answer, so I thought conferences and working late and went to the doctor's on my own.

ANTON: I told you not to come to the office anymore.

THEKLA: Because you don't want your colleagues to gawp at our private life, I know, but now I'm wondering if that's the real reason, and what's actually private. You said you had to work. Why did you lie to me? It's embarrassing.

ANTON: It was meant to be a surprise.

THEKLA: That you're lying to me? You left on time but you didn't use the door. Did you fly out the window?

ANTON: I left early and bought you a present. A present. So. So that's it.

THEKLA: A present.

ANTON: Yes. For you. As a surprise.

THEKLA: And where is it?

ANTON: What?

THEKLA: The present. Can I see it?

ANTON: No.

THEKLA: I think I'd like to see it.

ANTON: But you can't.

THEKLA: Why not? Because it's not for me. I'd prefer it if I didn't have to think you're lying.

*(ANTON leaves.)*

That doesn't mean you have to run away.

*(ANTON enters carrying a dug-out birch tree.)*

ANTON: Here.

THEKLA: A birch tree.

ANTON: I wanted to put it in the garden to mark the birth. By the pond.

THEKLA: A real birch tree.

ANTON: Yes.

THEKLA: The leaves are trembling.

ANTON: A diaphanous plant, too delicate for the harshness of reality.

THEKLA: Very delicate, those tiny leaves. You must hate me now.

ANTON: I don't hate you.

THEKLA: It was much easier to think you were lying and a stranger to me.

ANTON: Of course, suddenly the curtain is torn open and you see the terrible truth: I've stopped going to work and spend my days in cheap hotels instead, and kill time with magazines, or I sit in car parks and listen to the radio, I eat lunch in motorway service stations and don't drive back to town till the evening so no one sees me, or sometimes I take an exit and stand by a quarry pond or stop by the forest and struggle through the undergrowth, no one even bothers to ask why the sun burns my skin at my desk, apparently no one looks me in the face.

THEKLA: The things you come up with. I'd know.

ANTON: That's good.

THEKLA: I know this dear face, the heaviness in your eyes as if it was all down to you.

ANTON: How's the child?

THEKLA: The child's fine, she's sucking her thumb. That beautiful birch tree. I want it next to our bed tonight and listen to the leaves rustling.

## 12.

ASCHENBRENNER: The night is relatively calm. In the early hours of the morning there is a detonation, and shortly afterwards the water supply breaks down. While he is inspecting the burst pipes, the chief of command is slain by angry natives and his naked corpse dragged through the streets. The images are blurry, but it's easy to identify the faces, there's dust in their beards and on their skin and they look old. What we don't see is the massacre the soldiers wreak in the crowd before they throw down their weapons and run – there's no ammunition left and the rebels won't fall back despite massive losses, they push on in large numbers into the artillery barrage. At around 6:30 p.m. the western armies pull out of the northern part of the city. For the time being, they say, but the images of soldiers putting up an electric fence in the middle of the street tell me that the northern districts are lost. That means the economic backbone of our corporation is broken. My existence is ruined, I'll end it with the greatest possible decency, there are too many people I don't want to look in the eye after this collapse, myself included. I ask all of us for forgiveness.

## 13.

*(ANTON is sitting on top of the cupboard.)*

THEKLA: There he is.

OSKAR: He's in shock.

GRETA: I can see that, but what's he doing on top of the cupboard?

THEKLA: Nothing.

GRETA: Anton?

ANTON: Yes.

GRETA: What are you doing up there?

ANTON: Hello. I'm still a bit weak. The cat next door has caught the fish from our pond again. Now the water's barren.

THEKLA: He's dangling his legs and talking about his carp.

OSKAR: I don't care where he sits. Anton, can you hear me?

ANTON: Loud and clear: you said I don't care where he sits. But since it was a Japanese koi it matters a great deal where he sits, and you should really ask the cat about this.

GRETA: Anton, we need to talk to you.

THEKLA: You'd better come back tomorrow.

OSKAR: There's no time. Anton. It's very simple.

ANTON: It seems terribly complicated to me.

THEKLA: You can't talk to him, he's extremely upset.

ANTON: You can talk but you won't get an answer, fish are dumb. They open and close their jaws and swim back and forth in the water in total silence. You can stroke them, their firm, cold bodies, but do they notice? Hm.

GRETA: What on earth does he want up there?

ANTON: He's looking down at you, he's watching you swim and flap your fins. Here. Something to snap at.

*(He sprinkles fish food.)*

GRETA: *(To THEKLA.)* Your husband is definitely out of sorts. Oskar, get it over with.

OSKAR: Anton.

ANTON: They're actually terribly stupid, these creatures: when a hand approaches they greedily jump out of the pond, and then they lie on the grass and roll their eyes.

OSKAR: He's not listening. Anton, can you focus your brain for a minute?

THEKLA: Leave him alone, he's ill.

OSKAR: He can't afford to be. Anton.

ANTON: Look at the fat one folding his fins almost like he's trying to be respectable. Here.

*(He sprinkles OSKAR with food. GRETA laughs.)*

OSKAR: It's brilliant, Anton, all this stuff you're throwing at us.

THEKLA: Anton, what are you doing?

ANTON: *(To THEKLA.)* Nothing. You'd better stay clear of the battlefield.

OSKAR: *(To GRETA.)* Why are you laughing behind my back?

GRETA: The way you're tensed up in front of the cupboard waving your hands. It doesn't suit you: hysteria isn't very flattering.

OSKAR: Nothing I do suits you.

THEKLA: *(To ANTON.)* Please give me the can.

ANTON: No.

GRETA: And get the crumbs out of your hair, it looks ridiculous.

OSKAR: You should be glad there's someone in this room who's more ridiculous than you.

GRETA: *(To THEKLA.)* Now he's baring his heart so we can see it's an old mud hole.

OSKAR: Or does that diminish my appeal as a sex trophy? In that case I'm sorry, because then everyone can see that you're old and shrivelled.

GRETA: You're fast lowering the tone.

OSKAR: You'd better stuff me and hang me on the door so everyone can see you're still capable of attracting young men.

GRETA: You're hardly good for that, you pathetic wreck.

OSKAR: I didn't mean to be crude, it's just that apart from your money there's only thin, stuffy air in my head.

GRETA: That's all right as long as you look beautiful, you silly boy, so be good and get the crumbs from your hair.

OSKAR: You own me skin and bone, if the crumbs bother you, get rid of them yourself, I'll look after your money in the meantime. Anton. Are you listening?

ANTON: Every note. You want to ruin me financially.

OSKAR: Just pull your brain together for a minute, and after that I don't care if you go off with your fish.

ANTON: I never cared about those stupid animals.

OSKAR: It's a delicate matter, but we have to look ahead.

ANTON: When you look back everything seems smaller, have you noticed?

OSKAR: The way things stand now, we no longer have faith in the project.

ANTON: You never did.

GRETA: *(To OSKAR)* Very diplomatic.

*(To ANTON.)* I just want an expert to have a look at this.

OSKAR: It's too late, I told you that months ago.

GRETA: So now you can gloat, but please do it quietly.

THEKLA: *(To OSKAR)* I can't believe you want to talk about this now.

OSKAR: When else?

THEKLA: He's had a breakdown and needs rest.

OSKAR: Any later and it's too late.

*(To ANTON.)* There are rumours it was suicide.

ANTON: And I thought the mob killed him. Isn't that what they said on TV?

OSKAR: Aschenbrenner. I'm talking about Aschenbrenner.

ANTON: He's not the type. He's more likely to run amok and take a small town with him.

OSKAR: Apparently he hanged himself in the filing cabinet.

ANTON: I'd know. He doesn't even fit into the filing cabinet, Aschenbrenner deserved a normal heart attack and he got it, read the paper. There's a touching obituary – he earned people's respect and made a difference, and they don't want wreaths, just donations for the heart clinic. So.

OSKAR: Anyway, the situation has changed. The complex is in the middle of the sector and you have to cancel the contract. That's why we need the files you've kept.

GRETA: I didn't say anything about cancelling it, right now we just want the files, then we'll look at the options.

ANTON: I can't cancel it.

OSKAR: Why? That's what it says: in case of natural disasters.

ANTON: The money's gone. Thekla and I are living off it.

OSKAR: Figuratively speaking. But we're serious.

ANTON: How else can you afford a house like this? With a pond and fish in it? Are you still hungry?

*(Offers them more fish food.)*
No? I'll have a bit more.

*(He eats some fish food.)*

THEKLA: No, Anton, not that.

GRETA: We're not getting anywhere, the man's got a fever.

ANTON: Right. Had it for months. The man's not well at all. But no one's noticed. And then one day I'm dead and you're still talking at me – you change my underwear every day and buy a wheelchair for my corpse because I can't walk anymore and push me to the table, and you're slightly annoyed that I'm not eating and disappearing a bit more every day. Before I disintegrate completely you might even call the doctor so he can look down my throat and give me an injection, and then he pats me on the back and twists my shoulder in the process and says: you'll be fine, a touch of flu. And you're reassured and put a hot water bottle into bed with my cold corpse and when my head falls off you put it back on and for now you fasten it with two bits of sticky tape, it'll heal.

THEKLA: I told you to leave him alone.

GRETA: I didn't think it was this bad, he was obviously very fond of him.

THEKLA: Like a father.

GRETA: Anton. I don't want to ruin you.

*(To THEKLA.)* When he can think straight: I need the files on my desk by the end of the week. Then we'll take care of the rest.

ANTON: I'm the rest, and with the rest we'll feed the fish.

GRETA: Right.

*(To THEKLA.)* Is he going to run the company now?

THEKLA: Probably. Who else is there?

## 14.

*(THEKLA is sitting at the piano playing the same note over and over again.)*

ANTON: Thekla?

THEKLA: Yes?

ANTON: I thought you didn't want to go near the piano any more.

THEKLA: That's what I thought, too.

ANTON: I like it when you play.

THEKLA: I don't.

*(She keeps repeating the same note.)*

ANTON: That note –

THEKLA: I know I'm a disaster. But it's getting better.

ANTON: That's not what I meant. You've been playing nothing but that note for hours.

THEKLA: I want it to grow, to stretch like a muscle. But I lied and it's not getting any better.

ANTON: Maybe it's too difficult to make music with one note.

THEKLA: Why bother dragging myself on stage if I can't get this note right.

ANTON: You don't have to go back on stage anyway, why are you thinking about it again?

*(THEKLA stops playing the note.)*

THEKLA: I don't know, I'm not supposed to ask any questions, but what's happening down there in that city, at night, when the light is green, I see craters being torn into the ground, and when the sun rises I realise it was a hospital and there's still smoke, why doesn't it stop now it's over, and right in the middle, close to the bus stations, is the complex that's casting a shadow over us, but I'm in a safe place and I'm not supposed to ask what we're doing down there now that I'm having a baby to go with the strawberry fields and the terry-towelling toy and the nursery, why your brain is down there, at dusk people drive through deserted streets in the wrong direction and the chief of command is a pile of bloody flesh, and Aschenbrenner's hanged himself and you're sitting on top of the cupboard, it makes me worry about your future and think about my job, because I might end up having to drag all of us out of this godforsaken hole, and the misery of the community centres is yawning at me.

ANTON: You were shivering as if you were in a cage with beasts of prey, I'm not sending you back there. Soon the families down there will be back in their gardens and they'll be holding drinks in their hands in the mellow evenings and looking at the sky while swarms of mosquitoes whirl over the hedges and swallows shoot through the warm air. Someone's going to rebuild those houses – if your mother won't then someone else will, we don't care where the money comes from.

THEKLA: A couple of days ago I was behind the curtain looking out the window and you were standing in the street behind the car, looking at our house, one hand resting on the roof of the car, eyes empty, as if you were waiting for a voice in your head to say: go in, as if you weren't sure it was your house, as if you were a prisoner of war coming back after fifteen years. I wanted to call out, but suddenly I was afraid that if I startled you and waved it wouldn't be you. For a moment a strange man was standing there.

ANTON: I don't remember.

THEKLA: I'm glad you're not sitting on top of the cupboard any more.

## 15.

*(ASCHENBRENNER is in the cupboard, knocking.)*

ANTON: Stop it. I'm deaf.

ASCHENBRENNER: Everyone's gone, you can let me out.

ANTON: I'm not talking to you, you're dead.

ASCHENBRENNER: But you are talking to me. Turn the key.

ANTON: I didn't hang you in the cupboard, you'll have to cope by yourself.

ASCHENBRENNER: The keyhole is big enough, I'll keep an eye on you. I'm offering you a future.

ANTON: Dead people can't talk. You're only in my head.

ASCHENBRENNER: But if you let me I can step out of this cupboard and change your life.

ANTON: You've already changed it, I'm talking to myself, because it's a crisis, what you did to me.

ASCHENBRENNER: Don't be ridiculous. You're wrecking your future.

ANTON: I haven't got a future.

ASCHENBRENNER: I'm your future. Let me out.

*(More knocking.)*

ANTON: I'm going to go to the door and I'm going to open it, because someone's been knocking at the door for a while now, so now I'm going to open it so the knocking stops, so the knocking in my head stops, I'm now going to open the door where the knocking is coming from.

*(He opens the door. MANUELA is standing outside.)*

MANUELA: I was just about to leave.

ANTON: If that's what you want.

MANUELA: I thought you were out.

ANTON: Right. Everyone's gone.

MANUELA: But you're in.

ANTON: Our house is empty.

MANUELA: Apart from you.

ANTON: So?

MANUELA: This is when I used to have my lesson.

ANTON: That's in the past.

MANUELA: Can I come in?

*(Enters.)*

ANTON: The piano stays shut, and so does the cupboard.

MANUELA: It smells nice in here.

ANTON: That's not possible, there's nothing smelly in here. It's the rhododendron.

MANUELA: You've no idea what's stirring inside me.

ANTON: Complete mystery to me.

MANUELA: Paradise lost.

ANTON: Big words.

MANUELA: I thought I had to throw away my crutches and learn how to walk, but then I realised I'd thrown my legs away, and now I'm amputated. I'll wait here for your wife.

ANTON: Bad idea. She doesn't want to see you. Very bad. And I'm not in good shape.

MANUELA: You have to help me.

ANTON: Fortunately, I don't.

MANUELA: I'm a mess.

*(She starts to cry. There's a knock.)*

ANTON: *(To the cupboard.)* Quiet.

*(ANTON fetches two glasses and alcohol. Pours during the following.)*

MANUELA: I'm going to throw my life away. I've already thrown it away.

ANTON: You don't know what your life is yet.

MANUELA: If I carry on like this, then I don't want to know.

*(A knock.)*

ANTON: Stop it.

MANUELA: Help me. I have no future.

ANTON: You haven't even got a past, child. You're obscene.

MANUELA: Talk to your wife.

*(There's a knock.)*

ANTON: *(Screams.)* Stop it now.

*(To MANUELA.)* To whom?

MANUELA: So she'll teach me again. You're trembling, you seem very nervous.

ANTON: Piano music gives her a migraine. I don't think she'll risk it for you. Here, have a drink.

MANUELA: You look like a ghost.

ANTON: Exactly, I scare myself when I walk round the corner. Maybe you should buy a window-box or move to the country, put turnips in the ground and build a chicken coop. This city's been on their list for a long time. They'll attack from the west, they always do the train stations first, electricity and gas, once they've wiped out the big factories on the outskirts in advance, they invade the airport, it's their deployment zone, if you stay behind you can watch the grenades tear apart the big avenue downtown and then you can look down into the canals, they blow people out of crowded department stores without prior warning, it's better if you're somewhere else when that happens.

*(Screams because there's another knock.)* Stop it, this is not the end, there's still some scope, it can get even worse, if you think this is the end you're an optimist.

MANUELA: Are you sure you're all right?

ANTON: No. Unsure.

MANUELA: I'm not thirsty now, I'm leaving, it's getting late outside, my time's almost up anyway.

ANTON: And the darker the night gets the harder they chase you, and in the end there is only flight.

*(MANUELA opens the door, THEKLA and OSKAR are standing outside. OSKAR is carrying a bag with live fish.)*

THEKLA: What is she doing here?

MANUELA: I'm afraid I had no choice.

THEKLA: Seems like you have no shame.

MANUELA: *(To ANTON.)* And please talk to her.

ANTON: Sometimes you get nervous and you shoot the rocket past the helicopter into space, and then you know that time is against you.

MANUELA: I'm off.

*(She leaves.)*

THEKLA: What's the girl doing here again?

ANTON: She's showing off with suicide talk. She's silly.

OSKAR: I'll go put the carp in the pond.

*(He leaves. There's knocking from the cupboard.)*

THEKLA: No sense of distance, that girl. She's like glue, I don't like it.

ANTON: *(Shouting after OSKAR.)* Why don't you go next door and put the fish straight into our neighbours' feeding bowl? Maybe they'll let me drown their cat in our pond in return.

THEKLA: You're so loud.

ANTON: Sorry, there's so much knocking I can't hear a word I'm saying.

*(The knocking stops.)*

THEKLA: What knocking? I can't hear anything.

ANTON: You can't hear anything?

THEKLA: No. What is it you can hear?

*(ANTON listens.)*

ANTON: Nothing. Now I can't hear anything either.

THEKLA: Is everything all right?

ANTON: Everything's quiet.

THEKLA: Yes.

ANTON: Quiet. I could stand here and not hear anything for hours – just your face and you in front of the window like this.

THEKLA: I can't do that, I'm already getting tired.

ANTON: It's like when pain stops. I've still got a tingling sensation in my body.

*(OSKAR returns.)*

OSKAR: The carp are mulling about.

ANTON: Isn't Greta with you? I thought you'd look in the aquarium together and catch the big fish.

OSKAR: Can we have a sensible conversation, is that possible now?

ANTON: I've worn my dressing gown for days and it's wearing me down. And I drink limp tea. Hit me with clear sentences, it'll do me good.

OSKAR: Greta is talking to various lawyers and she's waiting for the files. Until then she won't participate in any fish purchases.

ANTON: That's what you advised her.

OSKAR: She doesn't take my advice.

ANTON: Too modest, I still think it was you.

OSKAR: With those kinds of sums you can't avoid the official route.

ANTON: You're family. Of course I'm very confident and you can do whatever you like, but the fact is that you're bailing out of a project I hand-picked for you after a careful risk-assessment, I didn't make it easy for myself, I can't help it, but I'm hurt by your lack of trust.

ASCHENBRENNER: *(From inside the cupboard.)* Don't tell me you actually believe that rubbish?

ANTON: What?

OSKAR: No one is blaming you for the massacres we read about in the papers every day. We're simply worried about her money.

ANTON: All this excitement is pointless. I've got the money.

ASCHENBRENNER: *(From the cupboard.)* So where is it? Do you mean the wine you've just had or the carpet under your feet or the bed where you lie awake at night?

ANTON: I've got the money and I can pay it back into her account note by note whenever you want –

ASCHENBRENNER: *(From the cupboard.)* Oh really?

OSKAR: If that's true then I don't understand why we still haven't got the files.

ANTON: Only I can't do it that fast. They're complex procedures that take time. You don't have to go waving lawyers at me. We're family.

OSKAR: If everything is in order, then you won't mind a lawyer.

ASCHENBRENNER: *(From inside the cupboard.)* It's just that it's not in order, because chaos has taken root in Anton's world, a black fungus that's dropping spores everywhere, no matter where you look or what you touch, it's contaminated.

ANTON: Shut up.

OSKAR: Me?

ANTON: Don't listen to him.

OSKAR: Who?

THEKLA: What's up with you?

ANTON: This isn't about me, you don't have to torture yourselves because of me. If you haven't got the entrepreneurial instinct – I won't force you.

OSKAR: I know you're very much linked with the project, and I can understand that you're worried about your job. But Aschenbrenner is dead. You'll be running the company soon, you're a free man.

*(Laughter from the cupboard.)*

ANTON: Like a fish in the air and a bird in the water, exactly. You've worn me out. Tell Greta she'll get the files.

OSKAR: When?

ANTON: Soon.

OSKAR: Why not now?

ANTON: There are some documents in the office I have to get first.

OSKAR: At least give me what you have here.

ANTON: That won't get you anywhere, I'll hand the whole thing over in one go.

OSKAR: Tomorrow.

ANTON: Tomorrow it is. My ears are buzzing.

ASCHENBRENNER: *(From the cupboard.)* I suppose you're hoping you won't survive the night.

ANTON: And the cupboard stays shut.

*(He leaves.)*

THEKLA: He's still stressed. I'm really worried.

OSKAR: Shall I give you a neck rub?

THEKLA: Excuse me?

OSKAR: I really don't mind.

THEKLA: My neck's not the problem. I wonder why he's so upset.

*(OSKAR goes towards the cupboard, intending to open it.)*

OSKAR: Who was that girl?

THEKLA: What are you doing?

OSKAR: Nothing, just having a look.

THEKLA: You're not supposed to open the cupboard.

OSKAR: Never mind.

THEKLA: Why are you asking about the girl?

OSKAR: That face. Makes me think silly thoughts.

THEKLA: Silly in what way?

OSKAR: Do you think the files are in there?

THEKLA: No idea. What about the girl?

OSKAR: I just thought – since it was so important.

THEKLA: The girl?

OSKAR: No. That we don't open the cupboard.

THEKLA: I don't know what's in there, I don't care. The girl's my student, if you're interested.

OSKAR: That's all right then.

THEKLA: What's all right then?

OSKAR: I'd just like to have a look in the cupboard.

THEKLA: Why did you ask about my student?

OSKAR: I don't know, I remembered bumping into Anton in town.

THEKLA: When?

OSKAR: Didn't Anton tell you?

THEKLA: What?

OSKAR: I didn't know, I thought you told each other everything.

THEKLA: We do.

OSKAR: That's all right then.

THEKLA: Aha.

OSKAR: Yes.

(Nothing. OSKAR looks at the cupboard.)

THEKLA: You didn't finish.

OSKAR: What?

THEKLA: Apparently you bumped into Anton in town.

OSKAR: Weeks ago, right.

THEKLA: Aha.

OSKAR: That's it, don't look at me like that.

THEKLA: And something troubled you.

OSKAR: Anton is a friend, I don't want to get him into trouble.

THEKLA: What kind of trouble?

OSKAR: That's something between the two of you, I'm keeping out of it.

THEKLA: Out of what?

OSKAR: Your private tension, it's none of my business, I don't like being used.

THEKLA: There is no private tension.

OSKAR: That's all right then.

THEKLA: Aha.

OSKAR: Yes.

*(Nothing.)*

I don't want to take anything, just have a look inside.

THEKLA: Did he say there was private tension?

OSKAR: He didn't put it like that.

THEKLA: How did he put it?

OSKAR: He was waiting outside a fishmonger's and said he was watching lobsters in order to relax.

THEKLA: I don't know anything about lobsters.

OSKAR: It's not important anyway.

THEKLA: And why did you ask about the girl?

OSKAR: Silly thought, like I said.

THEKLA: I don't see any connection between the girl and the lobsters.

OSKAR: Then everything's great.

THEKLA: Aha.

OSKAR: Yes.

*(Nothing. OSKAR looks at the cupboard.)*

THEKLA: But you can see a connection.

OSKAR: I don't know, I don't want to say the wrong thing here, so I'd rather not say anything. I wonder if the files are in the cupboard.

THEKLA: In your mind the lobster and girl add up.

OSKAR: You see, that's why I didn't want to say anything, I'm the one who's going to end up looking like an idiot.

THEKLA: You already do.

OSKAR: What?

THEKLA: Look like an idiot. You've already talked too much and said nothing.

OSKAR: I know it's none of my business –

THEKLA: Exactly.

OSKAR: But why does the cupboard have to stay shut?

THEKLA: I want you to tell me, in short sentences, what this is all about, the lobster, the girl, all your silly thoughts.

OSKAR: You're making a big deal out of nothing.

THEKLA: I'll be the judge of that.

OSKAR: It's just that I was wondering – although it's really not important – why Anton's doppelganger needs a room in the hotel by the square.

THEKLA: In the hotel.

OSKAR: I mean, if he's really just interested in the lobster. But you're right, it's none of my business, I just want the files from the cupboard.

THEKLA: A room in the hotel.

OSKAR: By the square, yes.

THEKLA: Aha.

OSKAR: I'm going to open the cupboard.

THEKLA: Do what you want.

(OSKAR *opens the cupboard. It's empty.*)

OSKAR: Strange.

THEKLA: Anton doesn't have a doppelganger.

## 16.

ANTON: What are you doing in my forest?

ASCHENBRENNER: It was only a matter of time until you showed up here.

ANTON: I chose this place because there are no people, just a hawk circling now and then.

ASCHENBRENNER: You can't claim a whole forest to yourself. I've been hanging out here longer than you.

ANTON: I've been on the battlefield for weeks and never saw you.

ASCHENBRENNER: I ordered this field, put down the foundations, everything's ready for our big project.

ANTON: You're fast. I thought you'd still be in the cupboard.

ASCHENBRENNER: Do you think someone of my stature ever rests? We'll realise our vision in this place.

ANTON: You're forgetting that you threw me out the window and into the kitchen waste.

ASCHENBRENNER: You're tailor-made for this challenge. This place is going to be an open-air museum of mankind. In the old days they didn't find the men who had hanged themselves in the forest until the autumn, when the leaves had dropped and cleared the view of the branches, or one of them had a crutch and put it against the trunk, and the wanderer knew: there's someone with a crooked leg hanging up there. From now on, when you take the exit to the forest, there'll be a passport nailed to each trunk so you know who's up there, and if that's not enough we can put up their tax returns as well. Then the visitor can walk from tree to tree in our museum of mankind, arms behind his back, and there'll be feet floating around his head and gently stirring in the wind. Everything's ready. Now hand me your passport.

ANTON: I have a wife, we're having a baby.

ASCHENBRENNER: You're whining again. Here.

*(He gives him a clothesline.)*

ANTON: It's a clothesline.

ASCHENBRENNER: It was the only thing I could find at your place. Hang yourself out to dry. For short distances you can also use your tie, in case you want to copy me again.

ANTON: I'm not ready, I want to see my child first.

ASCHENBRENNER: Your wife, your child – it's only got a fake future, you're aware of that, aren't you? What's going to happen when everything collapses?

ANTON: I don't know.

ASCHENBRENNER: You need to be professional about this. Your passport, please.

## 17.

*(THEKLA, ANTON and ASCHENBRENNER are sitting at the table, there's lobster for dinner.)*

THEKLA: You've set an extra plate. Are you expecting someone?

ANTON: Extra?

THEKLA: Is Manuela coming round?

ANTON: Manuela?

THEKLA: I'm taking the plate away now.

*(She takes ASCHENBRENNER's plate.)*

ASCHENBRENNER: I wasn't really hungry anyway.

ANTON: I guess I was thinking about the child.

ASCHENBRENNER: Clever.

THEKLA: Sure. And? Do you like the lobster meat?

ANTON: I haven't tried it yet.

THEKLA: The lobster's from the square.

ANTON: Aha.

THEKLA: The shop where they pull them out of the water while they're still alive.

ANTON: So that they're fresh.

THEKLA: I stood by the window for a while and wondered which one would have to die.

ANTON: Yes. Lobsters make you philosophical.

THEKLA: You've noticed, have you?

ANTON: I would imagine. In the face of death.

THEKLA: How calmly they float on death row.

ANTON: They don't know where they are. They're happy.

THEKLA: Stupid animals.

ANTON: Let's eat them.

THEKLA: A shop on the square, you've probably been there.

ANTON: I don't go to the square very often.

THEKLA: Aha.

*(THEKLA gets up.)*

ANTON: Where are you going?

*(THEKLA leaves.)*

ASCHENBRENNER: It's going to get unsavoury now because you don't know when it's enough and instead you stare at your wife, who has no future. You could have been floating among the trees by now, with a fresh breeze around your legs, but you're a sentimental wimp.

ANTON: I can't hear what you're saying, you're just in my head, and you haven't even got a plate.

*(THEKLA returns with the birch tree, which she's cut down.)*

THEKLA: There.

ANTON: What's this?

THEKLA: Cut down.

ANTON: Who did that?

THEKLA: Me. I cut down the birch tree.

ANTON: No.

THEKLA: Yes. This afternoon.

ANTON: You wouldn't do that.

THEKLA: No, I wouldn't, but I did. You'd never lie or cheat on me either.

ANTON: No.

THEKLA: But you did. Anything's possible, like on the first day, and everything's assailing me and there's no shelter. It's possible for a birch tree to stand outside the window like an insult and I fetch the saw from the shed and cut it down so it's over. It rustled when it sank into the grass. Wasn't very loud.

ANTON: That's the birch tree for our child.

THEKLA: I know your ways now, the phone where I call you at the office every lunchtime and send you kisses, it's not in your office but in a hotel room on the square, I saw you disappear into it today.

ANTON: What, how do you know –?

THEKLA: How am I supposed to answer that when I don't even know who I'm talking to, I look at you and I don't see anything, you haven't got a face anymore, everything's gone, it's like you shaved the face from your head this morning. Then at lunchtime you disappeared into the hotel, I want you to explain that to me.

ASCHENBRENNER: You can't explain anything, I've reserved the oak tree for you, no one's going to understand, you're mine.

ANTON: I can't explain it.

THEKLA: Because you're seeing a woman.

ANTON: No.

THEKLA: A student of mine.

ANTON: No.

THEKLA: Then tell me what you get up to in there.

ANTON:  I can't.

THEKLA: Because there's a woman.

ASCHENBRENNER: Just admit it, doesn't matter if it's not true.

ANTON: No.

THEKLA: Of course it's a woman, what else would it be?

ANTON: Nothing.

THEKLA: You rent a hotel room for nothing.

ANTON: Yes.

THEKLA: And you think I'm going to believe that?

ANTON: No.

THEKLA: Then tell me why you need the hotel room.

ANTON: To hang out.

THEKLA: With a woman.

ANTON: No.

THEKLA: Yes. With a woman. It's terrible: it all adds up, the last couple of months, you acting erratic, that you don't speak for days on end, it all makes sense now.

ANTON: It makes sense, but it's nonsense.

THEKLA: And the way my student has changed. I'm almost relieved now that I know.

ANTON: You don't know anything, everything you're thinking is wrong.

THEKLA: Then tell me what's right.

ANTON: I can't.

THEKLA: Because I'm right.

ANTON: No.

THEKLA: So it is my student?

ASCHENBRENNER: Admit it and that's it.

ANTON: No.

THEKLA: Why did you meet here when you've got the hotel room? Wasn't once a day enough?

ANTON: I'm always alone in that room.

THEKLA: Why?

ANTON: I can't tell you that.

THEKLA: Because you're with a woman.

ASCHENBRENNER: Admit it, or do you want to slam the fork into your throat while she's watching?

ANTON: No.

THEKLA: Yes. Why do you need a hotel room in bright daylight?

ANTON: I can't tell you.

THEKLA: Because I'm right.

ANTON: Please, don't ask me to explain.

THEKLA: You can stop trying to explain, it's clear as daylight.

ANTON: I've got the room against the rain. When I've been outside and walking for hours I get tired, once I stopped in the car park in the industrial estate and fell into a deep sleep behind the wheel, and when I woke up there was a beaten-up face with a pasty forehead pressed against the window, and it was staring in at me with inflamed eyes, so I went to the hotel.

THEKLA: A pasty face. Aha.

*(There's a knock.)*

ANTON: Exactly, I lost my job on the twentieth of March, and I have to go somewhere, I like spending time in the forest when the sun shines through the leaves, sometimes I'm there for hours watching hawks, but I'm a human being and I need a room when it rains, the noise when the key turns in the lock, the locked door. That's why I need a hotel.

THEKLA: That's the most ridiculous thing I've ever heard.

ANTON: It really is ridiculous, that's why I never told you, but now you know. No woman, there's only you.

THEKLA: We could have talked about everything, I'm fond of you and I'm having your baby. But you keep on lying, as if things weren't bad enough, it's obvious that you're cheating on me,

*(She starts to cry.)*

that you're telling me all this nonsense hoping I'll be stupid enough to believe you – you have to understand that I can't live like this.

*(It's still knocking, so she goes to the door.)*

ANTON: Don't open it.

THEKLA: Why not?

ANTON: Please. I need more time.

THEKLA: What for? You're lying to me and I've nothing more to say.

*(She opens the door. GRETA and OSKAR.)*

OSKAR: We've come to get the files.

ANTON: It's not a good time.

OSKAR: It never is.

GRETA: I can't wait any longer.

ANTON: I'm indisposed right now.

OSKAR: Give us the files and we'll go.

GRETA: I'm not interested in your private situation, today I'm here on business.

OSKAR: What's the birch tree doing on the floor?

ANTON: That's difficult to explain. I'd like you to leave.

THEKLA: I cut it down, we don't need the tree any more.

GRETA: Your relationship has definitely reached a critical point if you've started dragging the garden into your house. I don't want to know any of this, Anton, I must ask you to give me the files, I'm afraid I have no choice.

ANTON: Can't you come back later? Can't you see that–

THEKLA: I won't be here later.

GRETA: There's no time for discussions right now, my lawyer is waiting.

ANTON: Just give me half an hour.

GRETA: I'm afraid we don't have that long.

ANTON: Then I have no choice.

GRETA: No.

OSKAR: The files, or we'll see each other in court.

ANTON: We won't see each other ever again. I'll bring this matter to a decent end. I'll go and get the files.

OSKAR: You'd better.

ANTON: Wait here. I'll be right back.

*(He kisses THEKLA's forehead.)*

THEKLA: Don't touch me.

ANTON: I'm sorry.

*(He exits.)*

OSKAR: Well then.

GRETA: Get rid of the tree, it's not civilised.

OSKAR: This whole thing is embarrassing.

THEKLA: Shut up.

OSKAR: I'm just saying I'm not pleased with the way things have turned out.

THEKLA: I said I don't want to hear anything.

GRETA: Be quiet and get the plant out of here.

OSKAR: Right.

*(OSKAR drags the tree outside.)*

GRETA: Here, blow your nose.

*(Gives THEKLA a handkerchief.)*

You look terrible.

THEKLA: Look the other way if it bothers you.

GRETA: Letting yourself go like this.

THEKLA: If I'd let myself go the crockery would be on the floor by now.

GRETA: You don't have to exaggerate. Aren't you going to eat the lobster?

THEKLA: Help yourself if you're hungry.

GRETA: It's a precious animal, you shouldn't let it go to waste.

*(GRETA eats. Nothing for a while. OSKAR returns.)*

OSKAR: Has he brought the files yet?

GRETA: He's still upstairs.

OSKAR: I'm glad this thing is over, it was too risky from the start.

GRETA: I know, we've been through all this, 'you should have listened to me, I told you', I've had enough.

OSKAR: It's about respect, that's all.

GRETA: Shut up. I wonder what he's doing.

OSKAR: *(To THEKLA.)* Shall I give you a neck rub while we're waiting?

*(THEKLA stares at him.)*

GRETA: You'd better check what Anton is up to and give him a hand.

OSKAR: With pleasure.

*(He exits. GRETA eats.)*

GRETA: Is there any wine left?

THEKLA: Of course.

*(She pours a glass for her. GRETA drinks and continues to eat. Nothing for a while. OSKAR returns, points with his finger.)*

OSKAR: Anton.

THEKLA: What?

OSKAR: He's hung himself upstairs. He's hanging from the ceiling with a clothesline.

THEKLA: Anton.

## 18.

*(MANUELA is playing the piano. THEKLA is sitting behind her. Only music for a while, then a mistake.)*

THEKLA: Start again from there.

MANUELA: Yes.

THEKLA: And calm down, your fingers are still too feverish.

MANUELA: I'm sorry, I'm nervous.

THEKLA: It'll pass.

MANUELA: Yes.

*(She continues to play. GRETA and OSKAR come out of ANTON's room, OSKAR is carrying two bags.)*

OSKAR: We're all set.

*(MANUELA stops playing.)*

THEKLA: Don't let them bother you.

*(MANUELA resumes playing.)*

GRETA: Your things are already in the car.

THEKLA: The piano as well?

OSKAR: We'll get the furniture later.

THEKLA: It's an instrument, not a piece of furniture.

GRETA: In any case, you have to get up now and put your coat on.

THEKLA: I have to?

GRETA: *(To OSKAR.)* Go and put that in the boot, we'll be right there.

OSKAR: Yes.

*(He exits.)*

GRETA: *(To MANUELA.)* You can stop, the piano lesson's over.

*(MANUELA stops.)*

THEKLA: Keep playing.

GRETA: *(To THEKLA.)* We talked everything through.

*(MANUELA starts playing.)*

THEKLA: Right, I'll come to your place and have a foam bath to combat exertion.

GRETA: For example.

THEKLA: And I'll have breakfast at lunchtime and wear a pastel-coloured dressing gown and hold a small dog on my lap.

GRETA: Whatever you want.

THEKLA: No. Whatever you want. You own this house. The garden, the pond, the piano, what I'm wearing, the protein in my body, the fat, the chalk in my bones: it's all paid for with your money.

GRETA: If it's an investment that helps save you now that's fine with me.

THEKLA: You bought our life. I'd like mine back.

GRETA: You can't afford it.

*(MANUELA stops playing.)*

MANUELA: I'm sorry.

THEKLA: What?

MANUELA: It's impossible to concentrate. If I have to try not to hear your voices the whole time, I end up not hearing anything and playing like a machine. I'm sorry.

THEKLA: *(To GRETA.)* I have to ask you to leave. You're bothering my student.

GRETA: Think about it. You have no future here. The place is contaminated with memories. It won't be long before the poisoned air starts to suffocate you. My house has warm walls and sunlight on the parquet. Don't be proud. My door is open.

THEKLA: Thanks.

*(GRETA leaves.)*

THEKLA: *(To MANUELA.)* I'm sorry. Start again.

*(MANUELA plays. Music for a while.)*

ANTON: Thekla.

THEKLA: *(To MANUELA.)* Keep playing.

ANTON: Thekla.

*(THEKLA goes over to ANTON.)*

THEKLA: I can hear you, Anton.

ANTON: Thekla, it's stopped.

THEKLA: Be quiet, Anton, everything's all right, you shouldn't talk with that throat.

ANTON: It's stopped.

THEKLA: You need to get some more sleep.

ANTON: But –

THEKLA: Keep quiet, you don't have to worry anymore. They just came by to get the papers.

ANTON: It's over.

THEKLA: We'll lose the house and everything, but you won't lose me. I'm not sure yet how it's going to work, but it will, I'm sure of that.

ANTON: It's stopped. He's gone now.

THEKLA: You don't have to think that anymore. We'll watch our daughter grow, and the bigger she gets the smaller we'll get, till one day we disappear and everything belongs to her. That's what it's all about, that's the whole purpose, and soon we'll be a part of all that.

ANTON: Aschenbrenner is gone at last. I don't hear him any more. Not a sound. Everything's quiet.

THEKLA: Yes. Quiet.

ANTON: Quiet at last.

THEKLA: You have to sleep now, we'll talk about everything else later.

ASCHENBRENNER: At midnight local time, the western armies abandon the city. A temporary measure they claim, a strategic withdrawal, but the images of soldiers pushing helicopters from aircraft carriers – in order to make room for fleeing comrades – leave no doubt that the area is lost forever. Today we're faced with a historic challenge: the development of several thousand square kilometres of real estate in hitherto uninhabited territory. The scientists will supply water, everything else – atmosphere, seas, lakes, rivers – will come: life has started from water once before. Because of the change in radiation, people will grow a skin of gold, and shimmering figures will move through cities of red stone, everything's red there, the whole planet, and there's not just one sun in the yellow sky, but other stars as well, they're moving in a vast, formidable system, and this old earth looks radiant in the distance, it's so beautiful and so far away. Here, history has entrusted the investor with a piece of the world that looks virginal in the glow of the morning stars.

*The End.*